W9-DEC-596

NATURAL
DISASTERS

Tim Wood

Thomson Learning
New York

BOOKS IN THIS SERIES

AIR DISASTERS

ENVIRONMENTAL DISASTERS

NATURAL DISASTERS

SEA DISASTERS

Cover
(Background) Many millions of people each year are affected by famine because drought-stricken land cannot support livestock or grow crops.
(Inset) Natural disasters come in many forms such as earthquakes, floods, and forest fires, which can destroy thousands of acres of land and put many lives in danger.

First published in the United States in 1993 by
Thomson Learning
115 Fifth Avenue
New York, NY 10003

First published in 1993 by
Wayland (Publishers) Ltd.

Library of Congress Cataloging-in-Publication Data
   Natural Disasters / Tim Wood.
          p.   cm. — (The World's disasters)
   Includes bibliographical references and index.
   Summary: Summarizes natural disasters throughout history, emphasizing the causes, the loss of life and property, and ways of lessening the damage.
   ISBN 1-56847-085-1 : $15.95
   1. Natural disasters — Juvenile literature. [1. Natural disasters.]
I. Title. II. Series.
GB5019.W66 1993
363.3'4 — dc20   93-8525

Printed in Italy

CONTENTS

NATURE'S FORCES UNLEASHED

Earthquakes, volcanic eruptions, floods, and hurricanes are all natural events. They become disasters only when they have terrible effects on people. The destructive power of an earthquake or a hurricane both fascinates and horrifies us. Natural disasters remind us all that humans have little defense against the gigantic natural forces that constantly change and shape our planet.

BELOW Each year, massive areas of the world's tropical rain forests are destroyed. This deforestation can lead to soil erosion, landslides, and floods.

STRIPPING THE EARTH

The conditions that turn a natural event into a disaster are often created by humans themselves. Cutting down trees for building materials or clearing land for farming strips away the natural vegetation that keeps soil in place. Heavy rainfall in these deforested areas can wash away soil, making floods worse and causing landslides.

OPPOSITE Kilaueau volcano in Hawaii erupting, throwing red-hot lava 600 feet or more into the air. The Hawaiian islands have many active volcanoes.

The earth and the air above it are warmed by the sun; the heat then escapes slowly into space. Many people believe that pollution from factories and automobiles builds up in the air and does not let all the heat escape. This steady increase in the world's temperatures is called "global warming." One danger that could result from global warming is that the world's ice sheets in the polar regions could melt. This would raise sea levels across the world. Higher sea levels would increase the danger of flooding in low-lying areas, such as Bangladesh. Some scientists believe that unless we work to stop global warming, up to half of Bangladesh could be under water by the year 2030.

Natural disasters are almost always worse in developing countries, which cannot afford to build defenses to save people and property. These countries do not usually have good television or radio networks, which could warn people in danger areas. Nor do they have modern transportation systems, which could evacuate people quickly and safely.

When a disaster does strike a developing country, the loss of life is great because most of the people live in flimsy houses. People are more likely to lose their homes and to die from starvation or disease, which often follow a natural disaster.

You may wonder why these people do not move away from the danger areas. Usually,

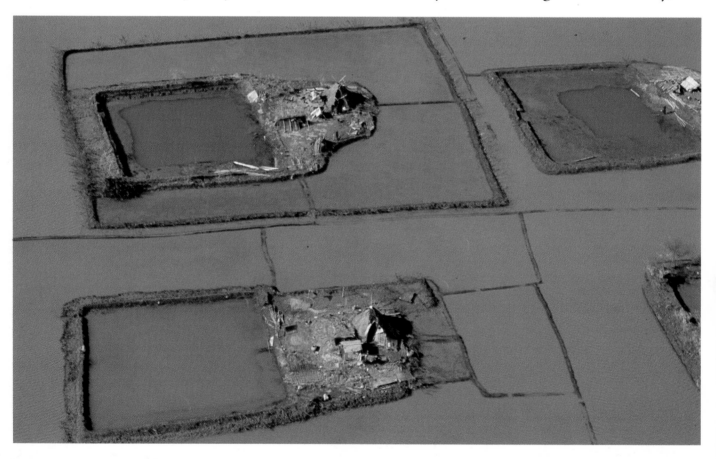

ABOVE Farms cut off by floods in Bangladesh — one of the countries worst affected by rising sea levels and deforestation.

DEATH FROM NATURAL DISASTERS	
TYPE OF DISASTER	% OF DEATHS
● Floods	39
● Hurricanes, typhoons, and cyclones	36
● Earthquakes	13
● Volcanic eruptions	2
● Tornadoes	1
● Landslides and avalanches	1
● Other (including forest fires, storms, snowstorms, heat waves)	8

the reason is that many of the developing countries in the world are also overpopulated (too many people live in them). This means that people have no choice but to live in areas where there is always the danger of floods, landslides, volcanic eruptions, or other natural events. There is simply nowhere safer for them to go.

AFTER THE EVENT

A developing country also takes much longer to recover from a disaster because its government does not have the equipment and vehicles to set up a major relief operation. The roads are likely to be in poor condition, so help takes longer to arrive.

International relief efforts may help to deal with immediate problems, but often natural disasters have long-term effects. Many years after the rest of the world has forgotten the event, the victims will still be struggling to pick up the pieces of their shattered lives.

BELOW Villagers on Sandwhip Island, Bangladesh, try to clean up after a cyclone in 1991.

WHEN THE EARTH EXPLODES

Volcanoes are openings in the crust of the earth through which gas and molten (liquid) rock escape. Volcanoes have been responsible for some of the most spectacular natural disasters in history. One of the great dangers of a volcano is that it can be unpredictable. It may lie dormant (inactive) for hundreds of years, appearing to be completely extinct (dead). People may live on its slopes, farming the rich volcanic soil, without giving the nearby mountain a moment's thought.

Under the ground, the main outlet or "vent" of the volcano may be blocked by a plug of solid rock, which makes the pressure build up until the volcano blows itself apart with a massive explosion.

A volcanic eruption is a spectacular sight. Often, red-hot lava shoots out of the volcano in a fiery fountain and pours down the side setting fire to everything in its path. Sometimes a volcano can erupt with such force that it destroys itself, covering a large area with rocks and ash. Most deaths from volcanic eruptions are caused by smothering in ash or volcanic mud, poisonous gases, or huge waves, called tsunamis, which are caused by an underwater earthquake or volcanic eruption. Often, those who survive the immediate dangers later die of starvation because crops and livestock have been destroyed.

LEFT *This eruption of the volcano Stromboli, on the island of Sicily, in 1972, showered the surrounding land with red-hot ash and lava bombs.*

POMPEII IS LOST

One of the most famous erupsions in history occurred in A.D. 79 when the volcano Mount Vesuvius, in Italy, erupted. It destroyed the nearby Roman towns of Pompeii and Herculaneum, burying the houses and more than 20,000 people under ash and mud.

ABOVE The ancient city of Pompeii, now cleared of the ash that buried it, has become a major tourist attraction.

FAMOUS ERUPTIONS

(A.D .79) Mount Vesuvius, Italy: 20,000 people in the towns of Herculaneum and Pompeii buried under ash and mud.

(1669) Mount Etna, Sicily, Italy: 20,000 people killed in earthquakes, which accompanied the eruption.

(1783) Mount Laki, Iceland: 10,000 people killed by poisonous gas and by the famine that followed the eruption.

(1792) Mount Unzen, Kyushu, Japan: 10,000 people killed.

(1815) Tambora, Sumbawa, Indonesia: 50,000 people killed by tsunamis and famine.

(1883) Krakatoa, Indonesia: 36,400 people killed by tsunamis.

(1902) Mount Pelée, Martinique: 30,000 people killed by hot ash and poisonous gas.

(1919) Kelud, Java, Indonesia: 5,500 people killed by mud flow.

(1980) Mount St. Helens, Washington: 60 people killed by hot ash.

(1985) Nevada del Ruiz, Colombia: 22,000 people killed by mud flow.

(1986) Lake Nyos, Cameroon: 1,700 people killed by a giant bubble of poisonous gas from the lake that had formed in the crater of the volcano.

THE GREATEST ERUPTION – TAMBORA, INDONESIA (1815)

This was the largest volcanic eruption in history. Nearly 50 cubic miles of ash and rock were hurled into the sky and blown around the earth, darkening the sky and changing the weather all over the world. In the United States, the following year, 1816, was sometimes called "eighteen hundred and froze to death" because of extraordinary weather changes, including snowfall in midsummer.

KRAKATOA – THE BIG BANG

One of the most famous volcanic eruptions destroyed Krakatoa in 1883.

Krakatoa was a small island off the coast of Sumatra in Indonesia. The island was made up of the peaks of three dormant volcanoes. The volcanoes had not erupted for over 200 years, but inside them massive forces were building up. The first signs of the disaster to come were a series of small explosions and a large column of ash and steam, which towered over the island. On the morning of August 27, 1883, the island exploded, blowing itself to pieces with the force of an atomic bomb. The noise, the loudest sound in modern history, was heard 3,000 miles away in Australia.

Lava, which reached temperatures of over 1,800°F, and balls of red-hot, sticky material called lava bombs rained down on the surrounding sea. A giant cloud of ash was hurled into the air, darkening the skies for hundreds of miles – for two and a half days. The eruption caused a series of enormous tsunamis that were over 100 feet high. These giant waves swamped nearby islands, washing away hundreds of villages and drowning at least 36,380 people.

BELOW This rare photograph, taken from a hillside on a neighboring island, shows Krakatoa exploding.

RIGHT A cross section of a volcano

CRATER

CRUST

MOLTEN ROCK

MAGMA CHAMBER

HOT ASH

ASH FALL

HOT MOLTEN LAVA

MAIN VENT

ROCK STRATA

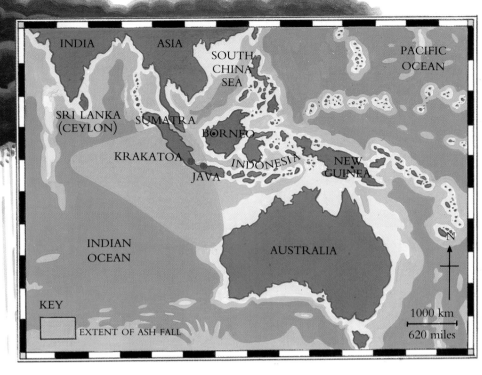

INDIA ASIA SOUTH CHINA SEA PACIFIC OCEAN

SRI LANKA (CEYLON) SUMATRA BORNEO

KRAKATOA INDONESIA NEW GUINEA

JAVA

INDIAN OCEAN AUSTRALIA

N

KEY

EXTENT OF ASH FALL

1000 km
620 miles

ABOVE A map showing the area affected by the explosion of Krakatoa in 1883

WITNESS REPORT

KRAKATOA'S GIANT WAVES

Eyewitness report by Mr. N. van Sandick, an engineer on board the ship *Loudon*, which was sailing off the coast of Sumatra:

Suddenly we saw a gigantic wave...advancing...with considerable speed...the ship had just enough time to meet with the wave from the front...we were lifted up with a dizzy rapidity...and immediately afterwards we felt as though we had plunged into the abyss...another three waves of colossal size appeared. And before our eyes this terrifying upheaval of the sea...consumed in one instant the ruin of the town; the lighthouse fell in one piece, and all the houses of the town were swept away...There, where a few moments ago lived the town of Telok Betong, was nothing but the open sea.

Source: *Krakatoa* by Rupert Furneaux (London: Martin Secker and Warburg Ltd., 1965).

MOUNT PELÉE

At 7:49 A.M. on May 8, 1902, the people of the town of St. Pierre in Martinique were starting a new day. All of the 30,000 inhabitants must have heard loud explosions as Mount Pelée, the volcano that lay just over five and one-half miles to the northeast, blew itself apart – but only two of them lived to tell the tale. A glowing cloud of gases and red-hot ash burst out of the volcano and shot down the slopes at over 150 mph. The fiery blast, called a *nuée ardente*, lasted only three or four minutes; but it shriveled, smothered, or set fire to everything it touched. The only two survivors in St. Pierre were a shoemaker and a murderer who was locked up in the town's jail.

WITNESS REPORT

MOUNT PELÉE DESTROYS ST. PIERRE

Eyewitness report by Assistant Purser Thomson, an officer on the ship *Roraima* sailing near Martinique:

I saw St. Pierre destroyed. The city was blotted out by one great flash of fire…As we approached St. Pierre, we could distinguish the rolling and leaping of red flames that belched from the mountain in huge volumes and gushed into the sky. Enormous clouds of black smoke hung over the volcano… There was a constant muffled roar. There was a tremendous explosion about 7:45 A.M. …The mountain was blown to pieces.

RIGHT *This photograph shows the ruins of the town of St. Pierre after the eruption of Mount Pelée. Everything in the area was destroyed by fire and only two people survived the disaster.*

LEFT *This photograph shows the cloud of gases and hot ash, called a* nuée ardente, *pouring out of Mount Pelée just before the eruption in 1902.*

There was no warning. The side of the volcano was ripped out and there was hurled straight toward us a solid wall of flame. It sounded like a thousand cannons. The wave of fire was on us and over us like a flash of lightning. It was like a hurricane of fire. I saw it strike the cable steamship Grappler *broadside on, and capsize her. From end to end she burst into flames and then sank. The fire rolled in a mass straight down on St. Pierre…The town vanished before our eyes.*
Source: *Volcanoes* by K. Wilcoxson (London: Cassell PLC, 1967).

RIGHT During Mount Etna's eruptions in 1992, barriers were built, using bulldozers, to protect houses and redirect the lava.

PREDICTING AN ERUPTION

It is not possible to stop volcanoes from erupting, so scientists concentrate on studying them and trying to predict when they could become dangerous. The scientists who study volcanoes are called volcanologists.

Using special heat-proof clothing, volcanologists sample the lava and take measurements with sensitive instruments such as lasers. When magma pushes up from inside the volcano it can cause the sides to bulge. Volcanologists measure these bulges with machines called tiltmeters. There are often small earthquakes before an eruption. They can be recorded by special machines called seismometers. Volcanologists have had some success in predicting eruptions using these methods. When an eruption does take place, lava flows that threaten houses can be redirected with explosives and dikes built from concrete and lava. When Mount Etna, in Italy, erupted in April 1992 all these methods were used to prevent the lava flow from smothering the surrounding villages.

EARTHQUAKE!

Earthquakes are caused by movements that occur at the edges of the giant plates that make up the earth's crust. These plates float on the hot, molten rock of the mantle below and are constantly on the move. As one plate slides past another, the rocks at the edges of the plates grind together. Sometimes the plates do not move smoothly and the two edges stick together until, with a great jerk, they snap past each other. This sudden release of energy causes an earthquake. Shock waves, called seismic waves, spread outward from the center of the earthquake, called the epicenter. The deeper the epicenter, the farther the shock waves travel, causing damage over a wide area.

EARTHQUAKE – CHILE (1960)

Chile, in South America, experiences frequent earthquakes. In 1903, 3,000 people were killed; in 1939, 40,000 people died. The city of Concepción has been destroyed five times by earthquakes.

In June 1960 the most violent earthquake in modern times hit Chile, killing 5,700 people and making more than 1 million people homeless. The earthquake's epicenter was at Concepción; it measured 8.5 on the Richter scale. The tremors, or earth movements, shook down buildings, trapping hundreds of people in the ruins. Huge cracks appeared in the ground. The earthquake triggered landslides and avalanches in the surrounding areas.

LEFT Rescue workers looking for survivors pick through the rubble of buildings after an earthquake in Mexico City in 1985.
BELOW A child is carried away to safety.

Although thousands of people were killed by the tremors and the damage they caused, more died as a result of the aftereffects of the earthquake. Roads, railroads, and bridges were twisted or ripped apart, leaving stricken areas cut off from help. In remote places hundreds of people died from their injuries as they lay crushed or trapped under the rubble before rescue workers could arrive.

In many towns and villages, underground electricity cables and gas pipes were split open, creating fires that raged through shattered houses.

Reservoirs and lakes burst open, and water pipes were broken. The damage to the water supply made fighting the fires even more difficult. Sewage leaked into the damaged water system, leading to the outbreak of serious diseases, such as cholera and typhoid, in some places.

In many areas the land sank several feet. This massive shift of land created a series of tsunamis, which hit many coastal towns, drowning thousands of people. For several days, extra-high tides washed over the ruins of ports and seaside resorts.

——— WITNESS REPORT ———

CHILE (1960) – THE EARTHQUAKE BEGAN IN SILENCE

One newspaper reporter, Patrick O'Donovan, described the destruction:

The earth movements began in utter silence. There was no warning subterranean (underground) rumble. And then came the long-drawn-out appalling noise of wrecking, of tearing and falling and a continuous silly tinkle of breaking glass. Sometimes fissures (cracks) opened in the ground wavering for 100 meters (328 feet) in parallel ripples, imitating the waves on the seashore. And when it was all over the birds began to sing very loudly. And then there were fires.
Source: [London] *Daily Telegraph*, June 7, 1960.

RIGHT After the earthquake in Chile, in 1960, even those houses left standing were so badly damaged that they had to be demolished.

WHERE EARTHQUAKES HAPPEN

Almost all the world's major earthquakes occur at the edges of the plates that make up the surface of the earth. More than three-quarters of them occur at the edges of the Pacific plate. This area is sometimes called the "Ring of Fire." Most of the other earthquakes occur above the edges of the plates that stretch across Asia from Burma to southern Europe and North Africa. Areas such as Japan, Indonesia, and the countries that lie on the west coast of the Americas are especially vulnerable to earthquakes.

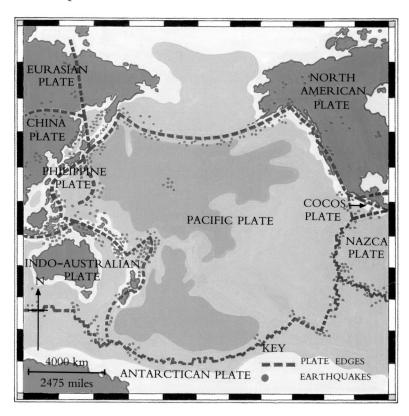

ABOVE RIGHT A map showing where earthquakes have struck around the Pacific plate area
RIGHT A seismograph measures earth tremors.

EARTHQUAKE PRECAUTIONS

Although scientists constantly monitor movements of the earth's crust with sensitive instruments, such as seismometers, they are not yet able to predict exactly when or where an earthquake is going to happen. Those areas that are hit most often by earthquakes have to prepare for the worst. Tokyo, Japan and San Francisco, California have both suffered major earthquakes in the past. These cities have been rebuilt to avoid further large-scale destruction.

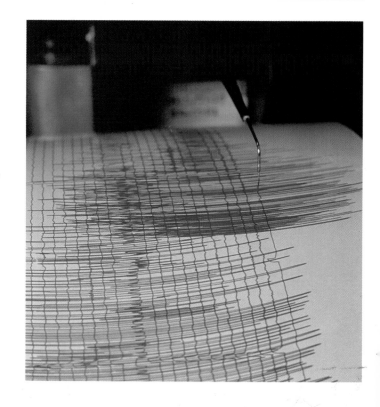

In Tokyo there are strict regulations controlling the size and design of buildings as well as the materials used. "Quake-proof" tanks of water and stockpiles of food and blankets have been prepared throughout the city.

The wide streets of San Francisco are designed to allow buildings to sway without crashing into each other. The wide streets would also help prevent the spread of fire after an earthquake. Some buildings have very deep foundations – some even have springs – to withstand the shock waves and tremors.

Even in underdeveloped countries, such as Iran and Armenia, houses in earthquake areas are now built with special reinforcements.

Other precautions include protected gas lines, water pipes, and electricity cables. Skilled teams of firefighters and rescue workers have been trained to respond to a disaster. They use heat-seeking instruments that can pick up the body heat of survivors buried under collapsed buildings.

LEFT Many buildings in San Francisco are built to withstand earthquakes. The wide foundations and base of the Transamerica Building make it much more stable when there are earth movements.

THE ARMENIAN EARTHQUAKE

On December 7, 1988, Armenia (at that time a republic of the former U.S.S.R.) was struck by one of the strongest earthquakes ever recorded. Worst hit was the large town of Spitak, which was completely destroyed. It was estimated that more than 55,000 people died during the disaster.

Armenia is a remote and underdeveloped country. Lack of equipment such as bulldozers and cranes made rescue attempts almost impossible.

Five hundred thousand people were made homeless – with only tents for shelter against the harsh winter weather. After their plight was reported on television and in newspapers around the world international relief workers began to arrive to help in the stricken area.

ABOVE In 1923, an earthquake almost totally destroyed the Japanese capital, Tokyo. The earthquake killed 140,000 people and made 1.5 million people homeless.

RIGHT Rescue workers shifting the rubble of collapsed buildings after the 1988 earthquake in Armenia

FAMOUS EARTHQUAKES

(1201) Syria: the earthquake that caused possibly more deaths than any other earthquake in human history. An estimated 1 million people died.

(1556) Shensi Province, China: an estimated 850,000 people died.

(1896) Honshu, Japan: a tsunami 100 feet high and traveling at terrific speed was caused by an underwater earthquake in the Pacific Ocean and drowned 26,000 people.

(1906) San Francisco: most of the city was destroyed by the fire that followed the earthquake.

(1923) Tokyo, Japan: probably the most destructive earthquake in modern times, measuring 8.3 on the Richter scale. In this heavily populated city, 140,000 people were killed and more than 575,000 homes were destroyed. The damage caused was estimated in billions of dollars.

(1960) Concepción, Chile: the most violent earthquake in modern times; it measured 8.5 on the Richter scale and killed more than 5,700 people.

(1976) Tangshan, China: the earthquake that caused probably more deaths than earthquakes in modern times. It measured 7.8 on the Richter scale and resulted in at least 240,000 deaths, although some estimates put the death-toll as high as 500,000, many of them as a result of the famine and disease that followed.

(1988) Spitak, Armenia: 55,000 people were killed and 500,000 people made homeless.

AVALANCHE!

An avalanche is a mass of ice and snow that breaks away from the side of a mountain and falls at great speed. Avalanches often occur in springtime as the ice and snow on the sides of mountains begin to melt. The most dangerous type is called a "dry-snow" avalanche. An avalanche of this type is made up of dry, powdery snow, which can form an icy cloud a thousand of feet high. This huge cloud of snow and ice races down the

mountainside at a speed of over 185 mph. Avalanches can be triggered by any disturbance, such as strong winds, the movements of a skier, or loud noises.

In 1916, during World War I, about 18,000 Italian and Austrian soldiers, fighting in the Dolomite Mountains in northern Italy, were killed by more than 100 avalanches, which were triggered by gunfire.

MOUNT HUASCARÁN AVALANCHE – PERU

The single most destructive avalanche in history occurred in 1970 in Peru. The avalanche began when 4 million cubic feet of snow were shaken off a glacier on the western side of Mount Huascarán by an earthquake. The huge, freezing mass fell 10,000 feet and crashed into the slopes below, setting off another 94 million cubic feet of ice and snow. As the avalanche raced down the mountain it picked up rocks, trees, earth, and other debris.

The gigantic mass roared into the valley below at 250 mph, engulfing the towns of Yungay and Ranrahirca, flattening buildings as if they were made of paper. About 30,000 people were killed – buried under ice, snow, rocks, and mud. The only survivors in Yungay were a few people who managed to run to safety in the town's cemetery.

Rescue work was made more difficult by the bad weather that followed. With roads buried under the snow and mud, the only way into the disaster area was by helicopter. Low clouds and rain kept the helicopters from

ABOVE This aerial photograph shows how the avalanche from Mount Huascarán swept away the town of Yungay, Peru. The circled area shows a high area of ground where some survivors were found.

landing for several days. The first rescuers to reach the stricken towns were 100 soldiers who parachuted through the clouds.

AVALANCHE DEFENSES

Many different methods are used to reduce the danger of avalanches. Sometimes explosives are used to release large masses of snow before they become dangerous.

In some known danger areas avalanche fences are put up and trees are planted to slow down or redirect moving snow. Roads and railroads are protected by concrete tunnels. Some ski slopes are closed during the avalanche season to prevent accidents.

SEA OF MUD – THE ARMERO LANDSLIDE

The town of Armero in Colombia, South America, lay high in the Andes mountains in a valley that was overlooked by the volcano Nevada del Ruiz. The snow-capped volcano had been dormant for over 150 years when, in 1985, it began to stir. A series of minor eruptions, which hurled rock and ash more than a mile, made the people of the area uneasy. But few could have guessed at the horror to come.

On November 13, 1985, the volcano began to shudder. Scientists who had been watching the volcano sent out a warning to the town of Armero, but very few of the people were willing to leave their homes.

Just before midnight, two loud explosions in the distance woke many of the townspeople. Some rushed to the town square. Others just went back to sleep. Unknown to them, high above the town, the heat of the volcano was melting its ice cap. An enormous mass of water, rocks, mud, and fallen trees began to slide down the slopes of the volcano. The massive landslide took about two hours to arrive at Armero.

BELOW *A sea of mud around the town of Armero. Only the highest ground escaped from getting smothered by the landslide.*

ABOVE *An eruption from the volcano Nevada del Ruiz set off the landslide that destroyed Armero.*

BELOW *The mudflow buried or tossed aside everything and everybody in its path.*

WITNESS REPORT

WALL OF MUD

Newspaper reporter Robert Tyler was at Armero at the time of the disaster. Eighteen months later he wrote the following description of the scene:

The wall of mud and water was 150 feet high when it slammed into the panic-stricken town in the black of night. Evacuation had begun, but too late. The horrific deluge engulfed 23,000 people, sweeping many of them away as they fled to high ground…It was impossible to tell whether the humps in this slime were cattle or bodies. But the tractors the wrong way up, the one solitary lorry (truck) *the right way up, all swept higgledy-piggledy across the land, show that no human being caught in the mud's grip could survive.* Source: *Sunday* [London] *Times*, June 14, 1987.

The landslide claimed 21,005 victims in Armero. The town and an area of 14 square miles around it were buried under nearly 50 feet of mud. The rescue operation was a nightmare. The mud was too soft to bear the weight of the rescuers or their heavy equipment. The only possible way of rescuing the victims was by helicopter.

Most of the trapped people who survived were pulled from the mud within the first three or four days. By the time international rescue teams arrived, few victims were still alive. Not many people could survive more than a few days partly buried in mud, injured and without food. Bodies of the victims continued to rise from the depths of the mud for at least two years after the disaster.

Most of the survivors now live in a new town nearby, which was built by the government. Every one of them lost a relative or friend in the disaster. Even so, because the mud could be turned into fertile farmland, it is probably only a matter of time before some begin to move back to Armero.

LANDSLIDE!
The worst landslide disaster in history occurred in Kansu Province, China, in 1920. About 180,000 people were killed by a series of landslides, which were triggered by a single earthquake.

ABOVE This dazed and mudcaked elderly man was one of the survivors of the disaster at Armero, Colombia.

OPPOSITE Rescuers struggled to save this child who had been trapped in the freezing mud for two days. The child died before he could be pulled free.

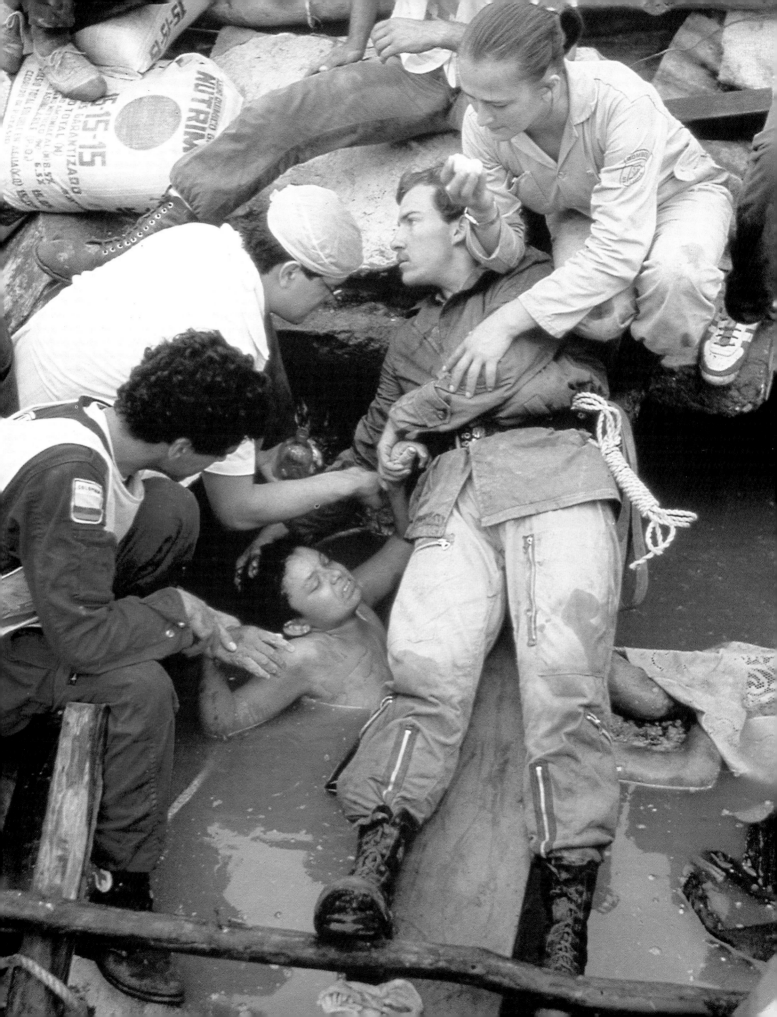

HURRICANES, CYCLONES, AND TYPHOONS

Violent, spinning storms – called hurricanes in the Caribbean, typhoons in the China Seas, and cyclones in the Indian Ocean – are probably the most destructive of all natural events.

The storms begin over warm seas. The sea heats the air above it, which rises swiftly, sucking in colder air below. The heated air spirals upward, gathering moisture and creating towering thunderclouds.

ABOVE *A photograph taken from space of a typhoon traveling across the Pacific Ocean*

The storm, which can be more than 1,000 miles across, begins to spin faster and faster and, driven by the wind, starts to move over the surface of the earth at speeds of up to 30 mph. At the center of the storm is a calm area, known as the eye. In a circle immediately around the eye, the winds can reach speeds of 125 mph.

As a hurricane moves across the sea it whips up huge waves, which can reach heights of up to 80 feet, creating a terrifying hazard to ships. As the storm approaches the land these waves, often up to 35 feet high at this time, begin to break over the shore. This is called a storm surge. The surge floods the land and destroys buildings and fields. It is the storm surge that usually claims most victims.

BELOW A map of northern Australia showing the route of Cyclone Tracy

STORM WARNING – DARWIN DESTROYED

Throughout Christmas Eve, December 24, 1974, warnings about the approach of a cyclone were broadcast on television and radio over northern Australia.

Few people in the port town of Darwin in the Northern Territory took much notice. They were busy getting ready for the celebrations the next day and believed, or hoped, that the cyclone would pass them by.

At 1:30 A.M. on December 25, Christmas morning, *Cyclone Tracy* hit the town with the violence of an atomic bomb. Winds of up to 150 mph smashed through the town, destroying over 90 percent of the buildings in about four hours. At least 45 people were killed and 10,000 homes were destroyed.

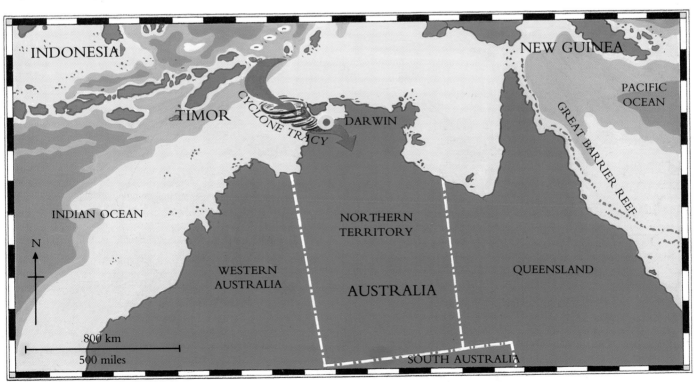

CITY WEATHER
Cloudy periods.
Est. max., 25C.
Yesterday's temperatures:
Min., 11.5C; max., 20C.
December 25 last year:
Min., 17.8C; max., 27C.
Weather Map, Page 55.

The Advertiser

Incorporating "The Register"

Family
Forum,
Page 41

Television, Page 45

Vol. 117, No. 36,237   56 Pages 8c   ADELAIDE THURSDAY, DECEMBER 26, 1974   Phone 51 0421. Classified only 51 0261

49 dead: more likely   **30,000 people homeless**   **All supplies of power cut**   **Food short, no fresh water**

CYCLONE FLATTENS DARWIN

At least 49 people are dead and hundreds more were injured in a cyclone which devastated Darwin yesterday.

CYCLONE TRACY DIRECTLY ABOVE DARWIN

A satellite picture showing cyclone Tracy centred over Darwin. It was taken from the Essa-8 satellite from 1,200 kilometres (745

City smashed to

Melbourne detectives drive British Labor MP Mr. John Stonehouse (centre) to the Federal detention centre in Melbourne yesterday.

Runaway MP wants to stay

From our Staff Representative

MELBOURNE — The runaway British Labor MP, Mr. John Stonehouse, who was arrested in Melbourne on Tuesday, wants to remain in Australia.

Three changes to England Test side

ABOVE The report in this Australian newspaper describes how Cyclone Tracy *struck Darwin.*

The cyclone simply flattened the town. Houses, made mainly of corrugated iron and boarding, were torn from their foundations and battered into pieces. Parked cars were blown over. Railroad engines and carriages were tossed about like toys. Telegraph poles were knocked over.

Several people were killed as the cars in which they were driving were plucked off the road by the cyclone and turned over. Others were crushed as their houses collapsed around them. Several people were hit by flying debris and jagged pieces of glass.

The 27 ships in the harbor moved out into open water to ride out the cyclone. Only six returned – some disappeared and others were driven ashore. One ship was picked up by the wind and blown more than 600 feet inland.

Bob Hedditch, the skipper of the prawn trawler *Anson,* had to lie on the floor of the wheelhouse as his boat rode out the cyclone. It was his engineer's first trip to sea. When the trawler returned to dock, the engineer left the ship and never went to sea again.

Most people hid in the rubble of their homes while the cyclone howled around their ears. Two-year-old Katherine Ginis spent six hours lying in a bathtub sheltered by her father while their home fell apart around them. At Darwin Airport, 50 airplanes were destroyed on the ground. Heavy rain added to the chaos, and to the misery of the victims.

The town was left with no electricity, water, fresh food, or working sewers. The government, fearing that typhoid and other diseases would break out, arranged for 36,000 people to be flown to safety. Police patrolled the town, ready to shoot any looters and thieves. After the people had left, the familiar sounds of the town disappeared. The silence was eerie. The dogs and cats

were shot to save them from a slow death from starvation. Even the birds left.

Compared with other areas that have been hit by strong winds, Darwin was lucky. Although the damage was estimated in the millions, few people died. The town was rebuilt and the new buildings were designed to stand up to cyclones. The walls were made stronger to guard against the impact of flying debris.

BELOW Darwin was totally rebuilt after the destruction caused by Cyclone Tracy. The new buildings have been designed to withstand the terrible storms that form across the ocean.

WITNESS REPORT

CYCLONE DESTRUCTION

This is how the scene after the cyclone was described by Gareth Parry, a reporter.

Darwin resembled a matchbox town crushed by a giant foot. Streets were littered with trees, smashed cars that had been picked up like pieces of paper and hurled for hundreds of meters, and the rubble of destroyed buildings. Source: © *The Guardian* [London], December 26, 1974.

RIGHT Most of the buildings in Darwin were totally destroyed.

AFTER THE STORM

Nothing can be done to stop a hurricane, cyclone, or typhoon. Instead, meteorologists try to identify them and plot their paths. Satellites in space take photographs of Earth, which are used to spot a hurricane forming. Airplanes with special equipment on board fly around the fringes of a hurricane measuring its strength and plotting its course. Weather stations throughout the world exchange information and use computers to figure out the likely direction of the storm.

All this information is used to warn people who live in the path of a hurricane, so they can be moved out before the disaster occurs. However, this is not always successful. If the predictions are wrong the hurricane may take a different course and strike somewhere else.

Sometimes, as in Darwin in 1974, people do not listen to the warnings or there is not enough time for people to leave the area.

ABOVE A meteorologist studying images from a U.S. weather satellite

CYCLONE DANGER FOR BANGLADESH

Bangladesh is a developing country, without many resources. It is also in cyclone territory.

In November 1970, between 500,000 and 1 million people were killed by a cyclone that hit a group of islands off the coast. Less than half the islanders survived.

One of the main ways to reduce the damage done by cyclones is to build stronger houses with storm-proof basements and strong shutters to protect the windows. In developing countries, however, it is not possible to build millions of new houses. Bangladesh has tried to solve this problem by building dozens of large cyclone shelters. These are similar to wartime air raid shelters. Each is designed to hold about 1,500 people but can hold more than three times this number in a real emergency.

The cyclone shelters are raised 10 feet or more above the ground so the people inside will be safe from the storm surge flooding, which usually follows a cyclone in this low-lying country.

BELOW The home of this Bangladeshi family has been destroyed by a cyclone.

LEFT Workers in Bangladesh building a cyclone shelter. The vertical steel rods are to reinforce the concrete of the walls.

HURRICANE HAZARD
– *HURRICANE ANDREW*, U.S. (1992)

Hurricanes are named alphabetically. The first of the season is given a name beginning with A, the next one B, and so on. The names are male and female in turn.

In August 1992, *Hurricane Andrew* swept across the South Atlantic and struck Florida with all of its might.

Leaving a trail of destruction in its wake, the hurricane moved on across the Gulf of Mexico and hit the coast of Texas.

BELOW Hurricane Andrew left a trail of devastation in its wake.

TORNADO!

Tornadoes are violent, twisting storms. They are like hurricanes but smaller and more powerful, and they move much faster. A tornado will usually form over land, in warm, moist air, where winds blow into each other from opposite directions. These winds create a spinning funnel of wind, inside which hot air rises at great speed. The funnel tightens to form a whirling column about 160 feet across. The wind in this column can reach speeds of up to 180 mph, and the tornado can race across the ground at 60 mph. As it travels, the tornado sucks up dust and debris, and the howling wind can smash the walls of the strongest buildings. Tornadoes can snatch up cars, airplanes, and even railroad engines and hurl them into the air as if they were toys.

As it passes over the land, the low pressure area inside the tornado creates a vacuum, causing buildings to explode as the windows are sucked outward. Anyone caught directly in the path of a tornado has little chance of survival.

BELOW The whirling, funnel-shaped cloud of a tornado touching down in the Midwest of the United States

WATERSPOUTS

Waterspouts are tornadoes that occur at sea. The whirling column of the storm picks up water from the sea and also contains rainwater from the clouds above. However, waterspouts are much weaker than tornadoes and last only a few minutes.

THE "PALM SUNDAY TORNADO OUTBREAK"

Tornadoes form in many parts of the world, but they are most frequent and most violent in the flat, central areas of North America.

RIGHT A rare photograph of a waterspout. Usually, they form for only a few minutes.
BELOW A map of North America showing the "Tornado Alley" area

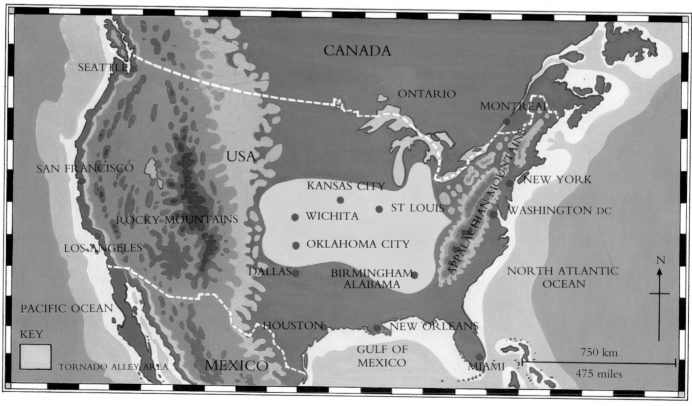

Parts of Kansas, Oklahoma, and Missouri are called "Tornado Alley," because as many as 700 tornadoes form there every year. Most of these tornadoes last less than ten minutes and travel at no more than 30 mph. However, there is good evidence to suggest that winds inside certain "super tornadoes" have reached speeds of over 600 mph. This is very hard to prove because scientific instruments, which might measure the speeds accurately, are always destroyed by the tornado!

Tornadoes often occur in groups called swarms. One of the worst swarms in

ABOVE This photograph shows a tornado traveling across Oklahoma in 1965.

American history, called the "Palm Sunday Tornado Outbreak," happened on April 11, 1965. In the space of nine hours, thirty-seven tornadoes formed in six separate states. A total of 271 people were killed. One of the tornadoes lifted an entire farmhouse 60 feet into the air.

The worst year for tornadoes in the United States was 1925, when 700 people were killed throughout Tornado Alley.

A GIANT SWARM OF TORNADOES

One of the most intense periods of tornado strikes in North America was in April 1974. Within the space of eight days, 100 tornadoes formed – racing across the landscape, cutting a path of destruction from Alabama in the south to Ontario in Canada. A total of 324 people were killed and 4,000 more people were injured. Some were killed by sand and gravel, which had been sucked up by the tornadoes. The gravel struck them like bullets. Some were torn to pieces or hit by flying objects. Others were stabbed by wheat straws that sliced into them like darts. After the tornadoes, such straws were found driven deep into the trunks of trees.

Although many people had been killed, some luckier people and animals were lifted by the tornado and put down some distance away, totally unharmed.

Two of the worst-hit towns were Xenia, Ohio and Brandenburg, Kentucky. Brandenburg was a small farming town of 1,600 people. The town had never experienced a tornado before and its inhabitants were totally unprepared for the disaster. In a five-minute strike a tornado smashed through the town, killing twenty-nine people and injuring many more. Most of the dead were children who had been playing outside their school. Three-fourths of the buildings were destroyed. Eyewitnesses spoke of cars, people, and even houses flying through the air. The disaster ripped the heart out of the small community and many of the survivors left, never to return.

BELOW *This town in Kentucky was badly damaged during a tornado strike.*

WITNESS REPORT

XENIA, OHIO – TARGET OF A TORNADO

When the swarm of tornadoes hit Xenia, Ohio, half of the houses were destroyed, twenty-eight people were killed, and nearly 600 were injured.

Many stores in the town were totally destroyed. One storekeeper, William Mitchcock, standing outside his jewelry store, described the strike.

"It hit at 4:40," he said, looking up at the clock in his twisted shop sign. The hands were frozen at 4:40 pm.

"We close on Wednesday afternoon…so I was away from the store at the time, but it passed just a little south of our home. It sounded like a fast passenger train. It was really just filling the air with stuff, really violent."
Source: *New York Times*, April 5, 1974.

ABOVE A store destroyed by a tornado strike

XENIA – A TOWN IN SHOCK

A reporter described another scene:

The storm cut a swatch a half-mile wide and three miles long through Xenia – all in five minutes. One terrified elderly victim, the roof of her small frame house completely blown away, sat wrapped in a blanket in a rocking chair…When firemen tried to persuade her to leave, she simply shook her head, refusing to say a word.
Source: *Time Magazine*, April 15, 1974.

PROTECTION FROM TORNADOES

It is impossible to predict the exact time and location of a tornado strike because the whirlwinds move so fast and can change direction unexpectedly. Meteorologists track tornadoes with radar scanners and issue warnings to areas that may be in danger.

There is no real protection from a tornado. People directly in its path have little hope. Most buildings in areas that are likely to be struck are built with strong cellars. When a tornado is in the area the people go into the cellars and hope that the tornado will not pass directly over them.

There have been many powerful tornadoes in the Far East. They are particularly destructive in India and Bangladesh, where millions of people live in flimsy houses with no cellars. These countries also lack good emergency services, which means more people are put at risk. The worst tornado disaster occurred in Shaturia, Bangladesh, in 1989 when 1,300 people were killed in a single strike.

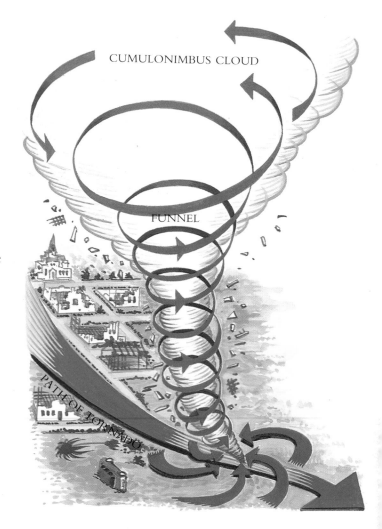

CUMULONIMBUS CLOUD

FUNNEL

PATH OF TORNADO

ABOVE A diagram to show how a tornado forms
BELOW Fragile houses in Bangladesh are especially vulnerable to cyclones and tornadoes.

THE MIGHT OF FLOODS

There are many different causes of floods. The most usual is a period of heavy rain or melting snow and ice, which cause rivers to rise and burst their banks. In coastal areas unusually high tides added to strong winds can cause the sea to flood onto the land. Storm surges created by hurricanes and tsunamis caused by earthquakes or volcanic eruptions can also lead to disastrous floods.

The collapse of a dam can result in great loss of life. In 1963, the Vaiont Dam in Italy burst, and the flood that followed killed more than 1,800 people.

FLOOD IN HONDURAS

On the night of September 18, 1974, *Hurricane Fifi* hit Honduras in Central America.

Although warnings had been given, thousands of people who lived in remote areas of the country either had not heard the warnings or were unable to leave. In thirty-six hours 24 inches of rain fell.

BELOW The Mississippi River flooded many towns, including Evansville, Illinois, in the summer of 1993. The soaked grain in the grain elevators will rot.

In the mountains, the streams and rivers began to overflow. Banks and dikes burst, and the muddy, brown waters poured onto the land. Thousands of houses and hundreds of the most fertile fields were swept away. Dirt roads, railroads, and bridges were washed away, cutting off many areas from help.

The town of Choloma was worst hit. Buildings were carried off and over 3,000 people and many thousands of animals drowned. Worst off were the old and the young who quickly became exhausted when they were swept away by the floodwater. The Honduran army collected the bodies, piled them in great heaps, and burned them. It was important to dispose of the bodies quickly to keep diseases from spreading.

The flood waters carried mud and other materials that poisoned the wells and rivers that supplied the drinking water. Honduras is a poor country with few helicopters, boats, or other emergency vehicles. Many of the worst-hit areas were remote, so rescue work was hard to organize. A huge international relief effort had to be launched. The final death-toll throughout the country was 8,000, with another 400,000 left homeless.

A GRUESOME DISCOVERY

When the flood subsided the dazed survivors discovered that the whole area was covered with a 10-foot thick layer of mud. Roads, bridges, and railroads had disappeared. Bodies lay everywhere.

One survivor, who had lost his entire family, returned to the wreckage of his home and discovered the bodies of two complete strangers there. He said they were "just poor innocents who were swept down the mountain and ended up here."

RIGHT *Survivors from Choloma cross a flooded valley.*

"CHINA'S SORROW"

Most floods are caused by rivers that burst their banks. The Hwang Ho or Yellow River in China is the greatest disaster area on earth. Over the last 3,500 years it has flooded more than 1,500 times and has taken more lives than any other natural feature in the world. This has earned the river the nickname of "China's sorrow." In 1887, one of the greatest flood disasters in history killed nearly a million people when the Yellow River burst its banks.

The reason for these disastrous floods is that the river flows along a channel that lies ten to twenty feet above the surrounding land. The rise of this channel is caused partly by the efforts of people to stop the flooding. They have built giant dikes of earth, reinforced with bundles of roots from a plant called kaoling, to hold back the river.

Unfortunately, silt (fine soil) is carried by the water and drops to the riverbed. Gradually the silt fills the channel and the water level rises. This forces people to build their dikes even higher. Over the centuries the riverbed has gradually risen above the surrounding land. This means that when the river does burst its banks, water can flood an area of thousands of square miles.

CHINA'S OTHER SORROWS

China has suffered flood disasters even greater than that of 1887. The higher death-tolls were a result of the starvation that followed the destruction of crops.

In 1931, over 3.5 million people died when the Yangtze River burst its banks.

In 1959, over 2 million people died in North China as a result of massive flooding which destroyed the rice crop.

RIGHT Floods in China in 1931. The townspeople of Hankow had to wade and row through the streets.

BANGLADESH IN DANGER

The low-lying country of Bangladesh is often affected by flooding.

About 40 percent of the country is no more than three or four feet above sea level, and disastrous floods often follow the cyclones that regularly hit the coast. Floods also occur when the Ganges or Brahmaputra rivers burst their banks as a result of heavy rain in the mountains to the north. Bangladesh has experienced five major floods in recent years. The worst was in 1970 when 200,000 people were killed by the tidal surge following a cyclone. The floods that occurred in 1988, when both the Ganges and the Brahmaputra rivers burst their banks, affected about 45 million people directly. Over 30 million were made homeless and 2 million tons of food crops were lost. At least 3,000 people were drowned and more than 100,000 caught diseases from polluted drinking water after the flood.

BELOW A map of Bangladesh showing the many islands and low-lying land, which are badly affected by floods when the rivers overflow or sea levels rise

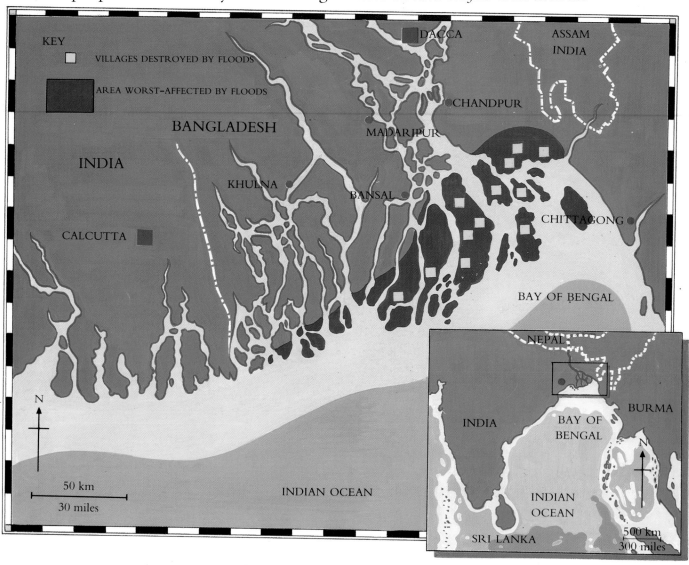

BELOW These children are carrying jugs of precious fresh water on their heads. After a flood, pollution and the diseases it brings often lead to thousands of deaths.

LEFT Fields and villages on an island off the coast of Bangladesh were flooded by the sea in 1991.

HOLDING BACK THE FLOODS

Flooding can never be stopped completely but constant monitoring of rainfall and river levels by meteorologists in many countries can help to give early warning of flooding to places that are in danger.

The most important guard against floods for countries at risk from the sea, such as Bangladesh, is better sea defenses. Unfortunately, building these defenses would be too expensive for a developing country. So, perhaps the only answer is international aid from developed countries.

More long-term measures, such as reducing the use of fossil fuels, would reduce global warming and could stop the slow rise of the sea.

DANGERS OF NATURE

There will always be natural disasters. The forces that cause natural disasters, such as the weather, the sea, and activity in the earth's crust, are much too powerful for human beings to control. In the short term, we can improve the ways we monitor danger areas to give early warnings; we can build better transportation systems to move people out of danger more quickly; and we can keep well-equipped teams at the ready to launch rescues and give relief. In the longer term we must reduce the damage we do to the environment and improve living standards. Only by doing these things can we reduce the human suffering caused by natural disasters.

GLOSSARY

Atomic bomb One of the most powerful and destructive weapons ever developed.

Cholera An infection that causes very bad diarrhea and can lead to death. The usual cause of cholera is dirty drinking water.

Crust The solid outer surface of the earth.

Deforested Cleared of trees, as the area of a forest or rain forest where the trees have been cut down.

Dikes Long thick walls of earth or concrete made to hold back water.

Evacuate To move people out of a dangerous area.

Famine A great scarcity of food in an area or a country.

Fertile (of soil) Able to produce a large amount of crops.

Glacier A slow-moving mass of ice and snow.

Lava Magma that has erupted from the earth, forming a volcano.

Magma Molten (liquid) rock beneath the earth's surface, or crust.

Mantle The part of the earth that lies between the core, or center, of the earth and the surface crust.

Meteorologists People who study weather conditions.

Monitor To keep a constant check on something, such as the behavior of a volcano.

Nuée ardente A red-hot cloud of gas and volcanic ash.

Remote Difficult to get to or out of the way, as in a *remote* village.

Richter scale A mathematical scale (from 0 to 10) which is used to describe the strength of an earthquake.

Satellites Machines in space that travel around Earth. They are used to collect information and send it around the world.

Seismograph An instrument used to measure and record vibrations within the earth.

Seismometer A seismograph that measures the actual movements of the ground.

Tiltmeters The machines used to measure any earth movement on the surface slope of a volcano.

Typhoid A high fever caused by dirty drinking water.

Unpredictable Changing behavior without warning.

Vacuum An empty space that has no air or gas.

FURTHER READING

Booth, Basil. *Earthquakes and Volcanoes.* New York: Macmillan Children's Book Group, 1992.

Matthews, Rupert. *The Eruption of Krakatoa.* Great Disasters. New York: Bookwright Press, 1989.

Walker, Jane. *Avalanches and Landslides.* Natural Disasters. New York: Franklin Watts, 1992.

Walker, Jane. *Famine, Drought and Plagues.* Natural Disasters. New York: Franklin Watts, 1992.

Waterlow, Julia. *Flood.* The Violent Earth. New York: Thomson Learning, 1993.

Wood, Jenny. *Storm.* The Violent Earth. New York: Thomson Learning, 1993.

PICTURE ACKNOWLEDGMENTS

Camera Press Ltd. 15, 34 (top) (Hoflinger), 38; Explorer 8 (K. Krafft), 22 (K. Krafft), 23 (both) (K. Krafft), 40 (bottom) (K. Krafft); Frank Lane Picture Agency 30 (top), 35 (W. Carlson), 36 (R. Steinau); John Frost Historical Newspaper Services 28; Impact Photos Ltd. 4 (C. Jones), 17 (B. E. Rybolt), 31 (B. Edwards); Photri 32 (bottom) (F Siteman), 33, 37; Popperfoto Ltd. 10, 41; Press Association 21; Reuters/Bettmann 39, Rex Features Ltd. 9, 12 (left), 18 (left) (SIPA), 40 (top) (M. Ginies), 44-45 (L. Chamussy); Science Photo Library 30 (bottom) (L. Migdale); Frank Spooner Pictures 6 (Bartholomew/Liaison), 13 (right) (E. Signorelli), 16 (Giboux), 24 (Bouvet/Hires/Duclos), 25 (Bouvet/Hires/Duclos), 32 (top) (P. Nucero); Tony Stone Worldwide *cover* (background) (A. Darling), *cover* (inset) (D. Austen); Topham Picture Library 5, 7 (U. Weitz), 12-13, 14 (both), 18-19, 26, 43 (P. Rahmantstr); ZEFA 20 (N. Gillette), 29 (Eugen).

All illustrations are by Tony Jackson.

ACKNOWLEDGMENT

Quote on page 37 (bottom): copyright 1974 Time Inc. Reprinted by permission.

INDEX

Numbers in **bold** indicate photographs.

The Body in Action

Thinking and Feeling

Jillian Powell

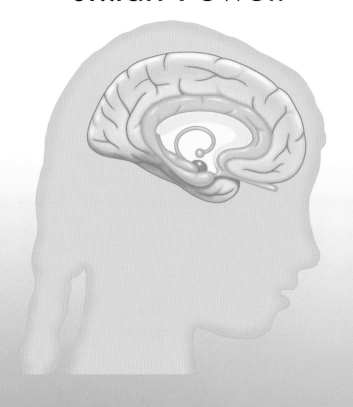

First published in 2004 by A & C Black Publishers Ltd.
37 Soho Square, London W1D 3QZ
This edition published under license from A & C Black Publishers. All rights reserved.

Produced for A & C Black by Bailey Publishing Associates Ltd.
11a Woodlands, Hove BN3 6TJ
Copyright © 2004 Bailey Publishing Associates

Editor: Alex Woolf, Designer: Stonecastle Graphics, Artwork: Michael Courtney, Cartoons: Peter Bull,
Picture research and commissioned photography: Ilumi Image Research, Consultant: Dr. Kate Barnes

Published in the United States by Smart Apple Media
1980 Lookout Drive, North Mankato, Minnesota 56003

Library of Congress Cataloging-in-Publication Data

Powell, Jillian. Thinking and feeling / Jillian Powell.
p. cm. — (The body in action)
Includes index.
Contents: How you think and feel—Your brain—Your nerves—Two sides of the
brain—Learning—Your senses—Using words—Remembering—Being creative—Feeling
happy or sad—Feeling afraid—Sleeping and dreaming—Looking after your brain.
ISBN 1-58340-439-2
1. Brain—Juvenile literature. 2. Thought and thinking—Juvenile literature.
3. Emotions—Juvenile literature. [1. Brain. 2. Thought and thinking. 3.
Emotions.] I. Title. II. Body in action (Smart Apple Media)

QP376.P6715 2004
153—dc22   2003060662

9 8 7 6 5 4 3 2 1

Picture Acknowledgements:
Corbis: Charles Gupton: 26; **Getty Images:** Benelux Press: 24, Tim Brown: 29b, Bill Hickley: 5b,
Geoff Franklin: 18, Michael Krasowitz: 16, Lester Lefkowitz: 29t, Elyse Lewin: 4, Photomondo: 22,
Mark Romanelli: 20, Frank Siteman: 10, Jacob Taposchaner: 28, Arthur Tilley: 5t, 6, 8, Ross
Whitaker: 12; **Pictor:** Jeffrey Rich: 14.

Contents

How you think and feel

YOUR BRAIN lets you think and feel. When you were a baby, you cried when you felt hungry or thirsty and you smiled when you felt safe and happy. Your brain was controlling these feelings.

As you got to know more sights and sounds, your brain stored the memory of these things so you would recognize them again. You learned how different things felt, smelled, or tasted. You learned to crawl and then to walk. You learned to understand words and to speak.

DID YOU KNOW?
There is no link between the size of your brain and intelligence. People with small brains can be as smart as those with bigger brains.

Babies start to smile when they are just a few weeks old.

Your brain controls the eye-hand coordination that you need to play games. Practice improves this ability.

During the first five years of your life, your brain began to store **memories**, and you began to think for yourself. You knew what your favorite foods were and what you liked to read or watch on television. You began to use your brain to do math, to understand how to play games, and to plan things to do.

When you hit a ball, your brain tells your body how and when to move.

Your brain

YOUR BRAIN is a large, spongy ball inside your head that looks like a giant walnut. It is soft and needs protecting, so there is a hard covering of bone all around it.

Your brain has three main parts. The largest part is the **cerebrum**. It is at the top of your brain and controls all your **senses**. In the middle is your **brain stem**. All the signals that pass between your brain and your body go through here. Behind the brain stem is another area called the **cerebellum**, or "little brain." This part controls the way you move your body.

Together, these three parts of your brain control how your body works.

Your brain is active even when you are asleep. It helps your body to grow and heal injuries. It also sorts through all the information you have taken in during the day.

DID YOU KNOW?
An average adult human brain weighs three pounds (1.4 kg). An elephant's brain can weigh up to 13 pounds (6 kg). A rabbit's brain weighs about .4 ounce (10 g).

This girl is using three different parts of her brain as she uses a calculator.

The cerebrum is the largest part of the brain. It controls your thoughts and **emotions**. You use this part of the brain when you think about a math problem.

The **skull** is a thick layer of bone that protects the brain.

The cerebellum, or "little brain," controls your balance and coordinates your movements. You use this part of the brain to move your fingers when using a calculator.

The **cortex** is the outer layer of the cerebrum. It receives signals from the senses and sends orders to different parts of your body. When you look at the screen of a calculator, the cortex receives the signals from your eyes.

The brain stem controls basic functions such as your heartbeat and breathing.

The **spinal cord** is a bundle of **nerves**. It carries signals between your brain and your body.

Your nerves

YOUR BRAIN is connected to your body by nerves. You have billions of nerves all over your body in a network called the **nervous system**.

Your spinal cord is your body's main nerve. It runs down your backbone, or **spine**, from the lower part of your brain. Nerves branch out from it and go all over your body.

Every second, your nerves carry millions of signals from your eyes, ears, nose, tongue, and skin to your brain. They tell it what is going on in your body and all around you. Your brain then sends out signals telling your body what to do. Some actions, such as eating or walking, you choose to do, but your brain also makes sure your body does other things all the time. It tells your heart to beat and your **lungs** to breathe—even when you sleep.

STAY HEALTHY

Vitamin B helps keep your nervous system healthy. Foods such as cereals, fruit, and green vegetables contain vitamin B.

When you shoot a basket in basketball, your nervous system first sends signals to your brain about the position of the ball, your arms, and the rim. Your brain then sends signals to move the right muscles.

DID YOU KNOW?

Multiple sclerosis (MS) is a disease that affects nerve signals from the brain to the body. The signals get weaker, making it hard to move.

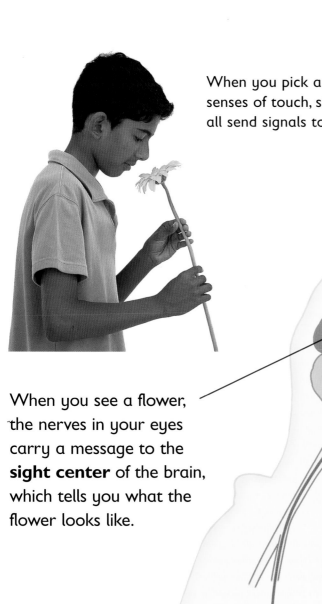

When you pick a flower, your senses of touch, sight, and smell all send signals to your brain.

The **motor center** of your brain sends signals along your spinal cord to the muscle in your arm. Your arm muscle raises the flower so you can smell it.

When you see a flower, the nerves in your eyes carry a message to the **sight center** of the brain, which tells you what the flower looks like.

When you smell the flower, the nerves in your nose carry signals to another part of your brain. This is the part that recognizes smells.

Two sides of the brain

THE MAIN thinking part of your brain (the cerebrum) is divided into two halves. Each side controls the movements and senses on the opposite side of your body. So the right side of your brain controls the left side of your body, and the left side of your brain controls the right side of your body.

Each half of your brain is also in charge of particular skills. The left half of your brain controls skills such as speaking and doing math, while the right side controls creative skills such as making art and music.

The two sides of your brain are connected by a bundle of nerves so they can exchange signals and information. For most activities you need both sides to work together. So, when you read the word "cat," you use the left side of your brain to understand the word, and the right side to picture a cat in your mind.

The right side of the brain controls creative skills for most people.

Both sides of your brain work together to help you complete a jigsaw puzzle.

DID YOU KNOW?
If you are right-handed, the left side of your brain is probably stronger. If you are left-handed, the right side is probably stronger. This may be why some of the greatest artists, such as Michelangelo, were left-handed.

The right side of your brain helps you imagine a puzzle as a whole picture.

The left side of your brain helps you figure out where the puzzle pieces fit.

Nerves deep inside the brain join the right and left sides.

11

Learning

TO LEARN, your brain needs to take in lots of information from your senses, such as your sight and hearing. It sorts the information, storing the bits it needs and forgetting the rest. It then tells your body what it understands from the information, and what you need to do.

Your brain is made up of 100 billion tiny **brain cells**. When you think, nerve signals flash between these brain cells. They travel at about 218 miles (350 km) an hour. Billions of signals can jump between your brain cells every second.

When you learn something new, the signals start to form patterns. As you practice your new skill, your brain recalls these patterns. Each time, the patterns become stronger and the task gets easier.

DID YOU KNOW?
Epilepsy is a disease caused by brain cells firing off nerve signals faster than usual. When this happens, the body shakes violently. This is called a seizure, and it lasts until the cells return to normal.

You learned to eat without having to think about it, but you need to practice other skills.

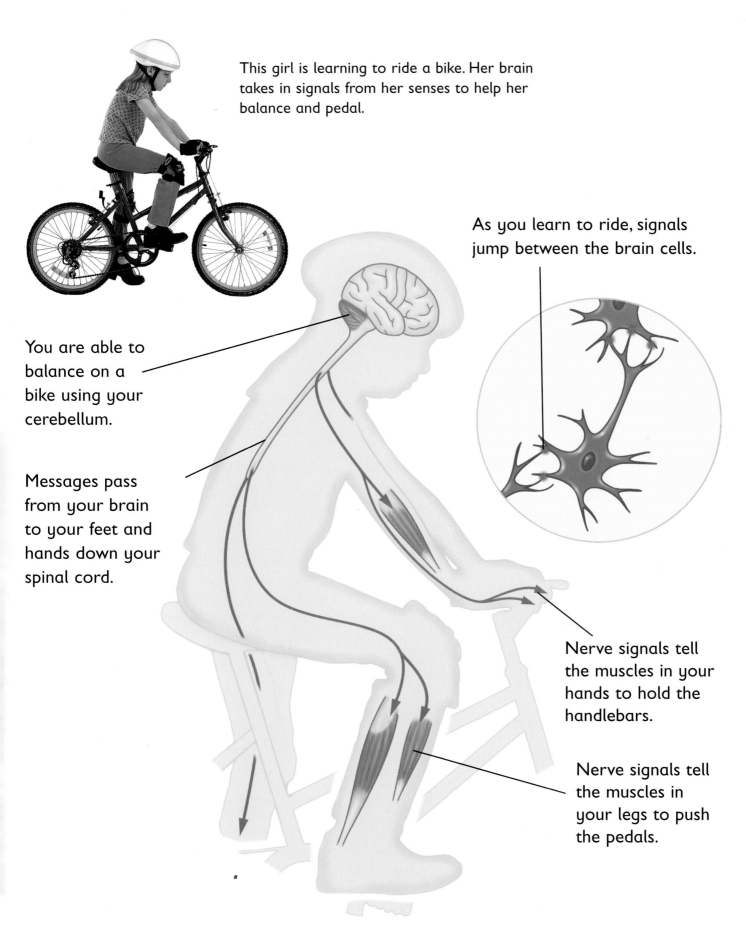

This girl is learning to ride a bike. Her brain takes in signals from her senses to help her balance and pedal.

As you learn to ride, signals jump between the brain cells.

You are able to balance on a bike using your cerebellum.

Messages pass from your brain to your feet and hands down your spinal cord.

Nerve signals tell the muscles in your hands to hold the handlebars.

Nerve signals tell the muscles in your legs to push the pedals.

Your senses

YOUR BODY has **receptors** in your skin that take in information from your five senses—sight, hearing, touch, smell, and taste. The receptors turn the information into signals. Nerves carry these signals to your brain. Part of your inner brain sorts all the information from your senses.

A small part at the center of your brain watches your body temperature and your appetite. If you feel too hot or too cold, it sends signals to make you sweat or shiver. If your body needs food or water, it sends signals that make you feel hungry or thirsty. Your brain also receives signals of pain when your body is hurt or sick.

When you feel cold, you shiver. This is because your brain tells your muscles to shake your body to warm you up.

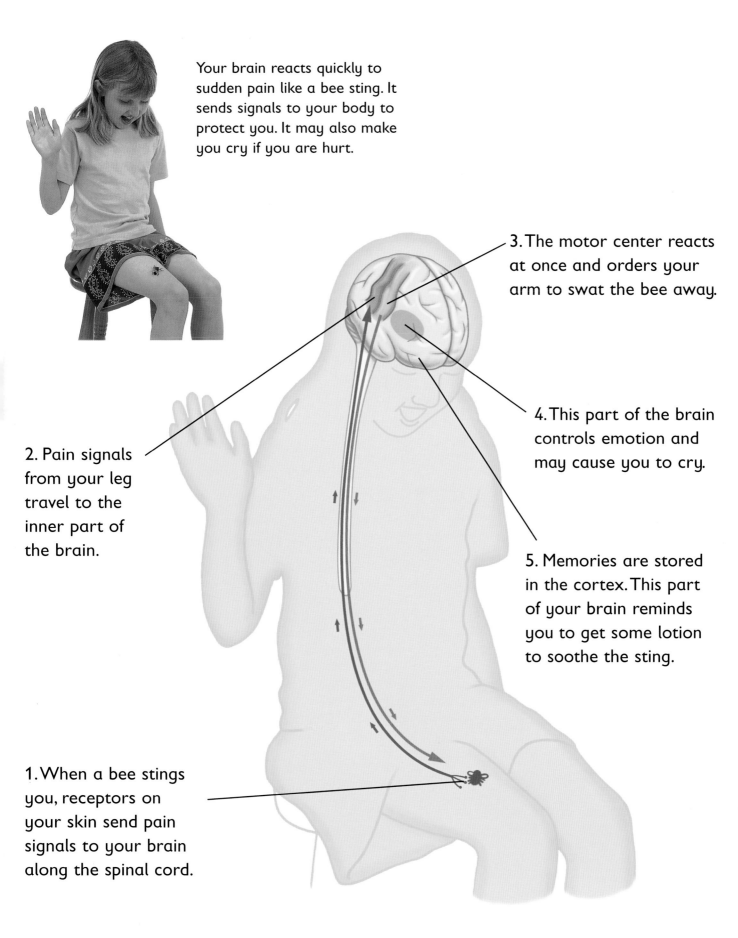

Your brain reacts quickly to sudden pain like a bee sting. It sends signals to your body to protect you. It may also make you cry if you are hurt.

3. The motor center reacts at once and orders your arm to swat the bee away.

4. This part of the brain controls emotion and may cause you to cry.

2. Pain signals from your leg travel to the inner part of the brain.

5. Memories are stored in the cortex. This part of your brain reminds you to get some lotion to soothe the sting.

1. When a bee stings you, receptors on your skin send pain signals to your brain along the spinal cord.

Using words

W HEN SOMEONE speaks to you, your ears pick up the sounds of the words and turn them into nerve signals that travel to your brain. Your brain then sends signals to the **speech center**, which figures out what has been said.

To speak, your brain uses the speech center to form words and sentences. It then sends signals to tell your **voice box**, throat, tongue, and lips to make the sounds.

You also use your speech center when you read. Your eyes take in the shapes of letters and words and turn them into nerve signals. They send these signals to your brain so that it can figure out the meaning.

DID YOU KNOW?
Singing is good for you because it increases substances in your blood that fight germs!

When you write, signals move very quickly between your brain and your eyes and hand.

DID YOU KNOW?
People who have dyslexia find it hard to read, learn, and write words because their brains mix up letters and words. Dyslexia may be caused by problems in the way the brain sends signals to its speech center.

When you read aloud, you use many different parts of your brain.

2. The nerve signals travel from your eyes to the sight center, which tells you what the words look like.

3. Signals are now sent from the sight center to the speech center of your brain. Here you make sense of the words.

1. First, your eyes take in the shapes of the words. They turn them into nerve signals.

4. Your brain sends signals to this area, where you figure out how to say the words.

5. Finally, signals are sent to your voice box, throat, tongue, and lips, which tell them to form the sounds of the words.

Remembering

YOUR BRAIN can store and recall ideas, events, and even feelings in your memory. You have two types of memory: short-term and long-term. Your short-term memory stores events that have just happened. Your long-term memory stores experiences from your past.

Your long-term memory will never become full. By the time you are eight years old, it can store more information than a million encyclopedias. It can go on storing new information throughout your life.

Each time you form a new memory, one brain cell links up with thousands of others to form a pattern of signals that you can later recall.

DID YOU KNOW?
Your memory is like a muscle: it gets stronger every time you use it. If you do not use it, you will eventually forget things.

When you are learning something, you use the same brain connections over and over again. You can recall patterns from your memory during a test.

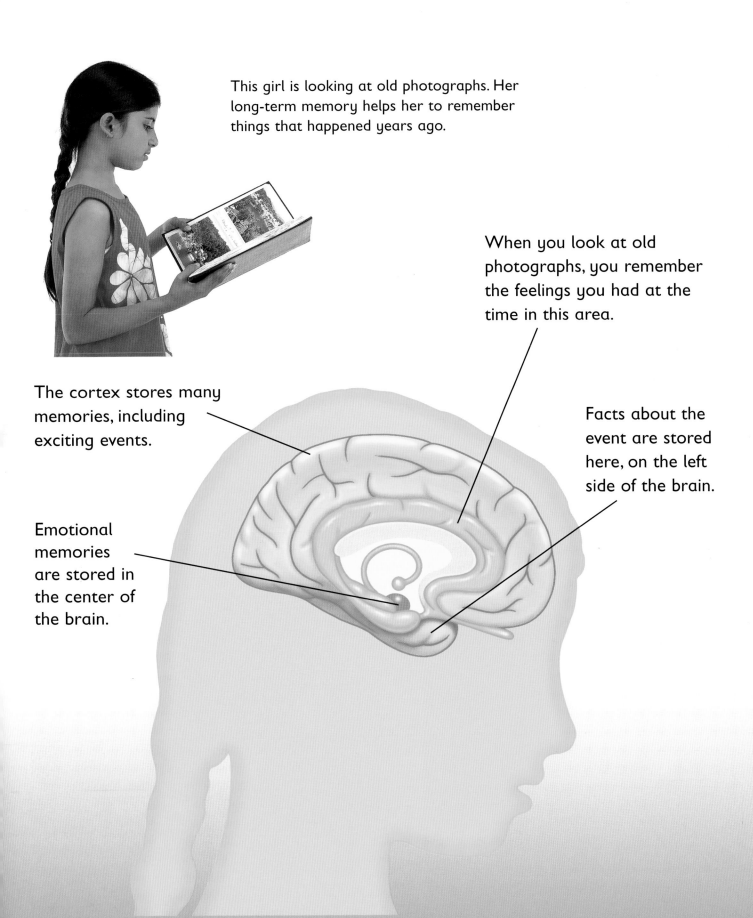

This girl is looking at old photographs. Her long-term memory helps her to remember things that happened years ago.

When you look at old photographs, you remember the feelings you had at the time in this area.

The cortex stores many memories, including exciting events.

Facts about the event are stored here, on the left side of the brain.

Emotional memories are stored in the center of the brain.

Being creative

YOU USE the right side of your brain when you are being creative. It helps you think about pictures or patterns. You use it when you are drawing or painting, playing a musical instrument, dancing, using your imagination, or daydreaming. It also helps you recognize faces, shapes, and patterns, and judge space and distance.

When you paint a picture, you use the thinking part of your brain to invent an idea. You may use memories stored in different parts of your brain. As you start to paint, your eyes send signals to the sight center of the brain. Your hands send signals as you pick up and move the brush. Your brain sends signals back to the muscles in your arm and hands, telling them what to do next.

DID YOU KNOW?

If you are right-handed, you can improve your creative skills by drawing with your left hand. This will exercise the right side of your brain.

DID YOU KNOW?

Your brain is unique. No two brains are shaped or wired exactly the same way, so we all have different skills and talents.

When you write a poem, you use different parts of your brain to find words to go with your feelings.

20

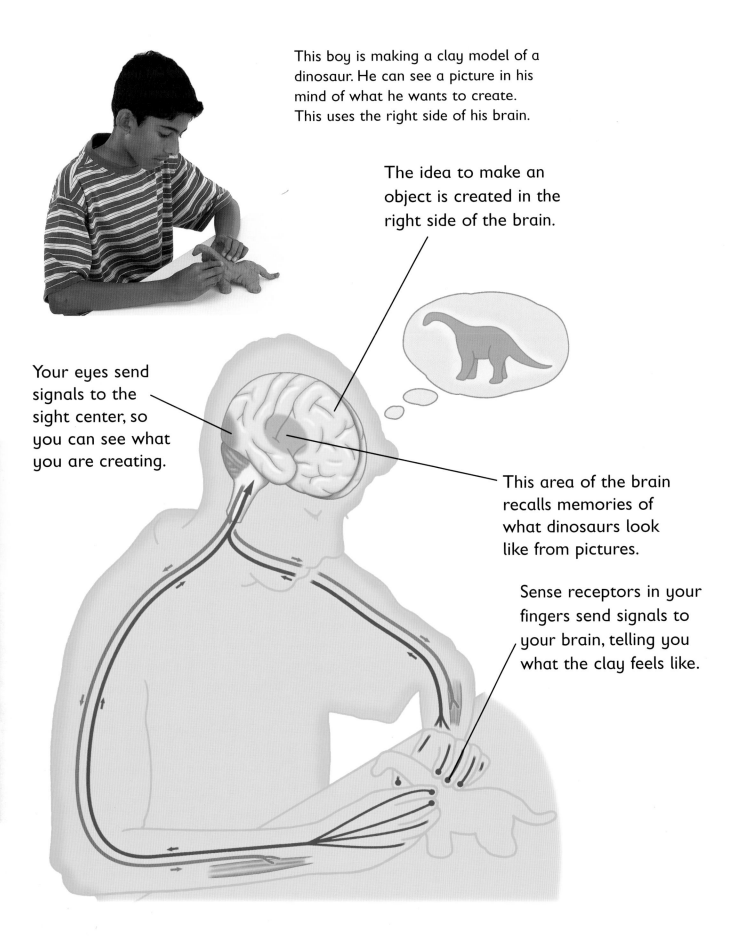

This boy is making a clay model of a dinosaur. He can see a picture in his mind of what he wants to create. This uses the right side of his brain.

The idea to make an object is created in the right side of the brain.

Your eyes send signals to the sight center, so you can see what you are creating.

This area of the brain recalls memories of what dinosaurs look like from pictures.

Sense receptors in your fingers send signals to your brain, telling you what the clay feels like.

Feeling happy or sad

W E ALL feel happy, sad, or angry at different times. If you win a prize or a sports competition, you feel happy. If you have to say good-bye to friends, or if someone you love dies, you feel sad. We call these feelings emotions. They are controlled in a special area of your brain.

Your mood is changed by chemicals in your brain. A chemical called **serotonin**, for example, can give feelings of pleasure. The chemicals pass from one brain cell to another and carry signals between them. This affects how you feel.

DID YOU KNOW?
Chocolate contains chemicals that react with the chemicals in your brain to make you feel good!

The way you feel changes the way you look and behave. When you are happy, you smile or laugh. When you are sad, you may be quiet or cry.

Scoring a goal activates chemicals in your brain, and you experience a rush of excitement.

When you see the ball enter the net, nerve signals travel from your eyes to the sight center of your brain.

Your brain then sends signals to this area, which makes you feel happy.

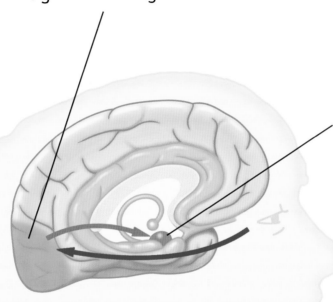

Feeling afraid

EVERYONE FEELS afraid or worried sometimes. Fear can make your heart beat faster and your mouth feel dry. You may even start to sweat. You sense fear with the same part of the brain that you sense happiness, sadness, and other emotions.

When nerve signals tell your brain that you feel afraid, your brain prepares your body for escape. It sends out signals to slow down your **digestive system** so you can use energy for other things. It tells your heart to beat faster to pump more blood to your muscles, and it tells your lungs to breathe faster to take in more air. Even the **pupils** in your eyes get larger so you can see well!

Your brain also tells your body to start making a **hormone**, or chemical, called **adrenalin**. Adrenalin puts your whole body on alert.

Adrenalin can help us in any situation in which we feel pressure. It can even help us do well in sports, but the effects last for only a short time.

DID YOU KNOW?
Scientists call our reaction to fear "fight or flight." They think it began long ago when our caveman ancestors were in danger from wild animals. They had to either fight or escape.

24

When you see or hear something that scares you, your brain tells your body to react fast.

When you are frightened, you sense fear in this part of your brain.

Your heart rate increases to pump blood faster to your brain and muscles.

The pupils in your eyes get larger to let in more light and improve your eyesight.

Your lungs breathe faster to take in more air.

Your body starts producing adrenalin, which puts your body on alert.

Sleeping and dreaming

Y OU SPEND about a third of your life asleep. When you feel tired, your brain sends out signals that make you go to sleep. Your breathing and heartbeat slow down, and your muscles relax.

During the night, you experience light sleep and deep sleep. Your brain is most active during light sleep: your heartbeat gets faster, your muscles twitch, and your eyes move rapidly under your eyelids. This is when you dream. Some scientists think dreams are your brain's way of sorting through experiences and memories.

DID YOU KNOW?
Children dream for 50 percent of the night, and adults dream for 20 percent. You remember only your last dream, even though you may have many during the night.

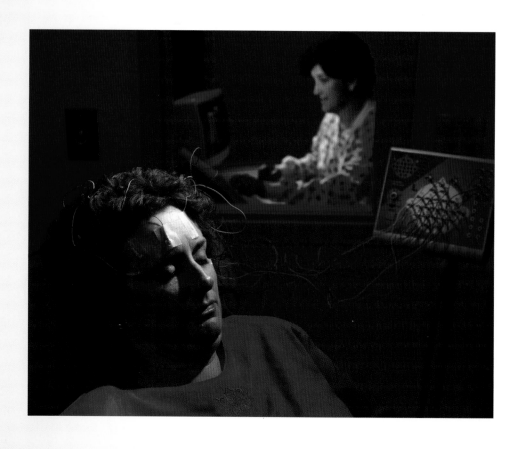

Scientists can watch a person's brain work during sleep. They use a special machine that records nerve signals in the brain as wavy lines on a computer screen.

Your brain and body need sleep to keep them working properly. This is the time when your body grows and repairs injuries.

This is the sleep/wake center in your brain. It sends messages to the rest of your brain to tell it when you need to sleep.

Your body sends signals that it is warm and comfortable along your spinal cord. They tell your brain you are ready to sleep.

While you are asleep, this part of the brain sorts information from the day and decides what to store and what to forget.

Caring for your brain

EXERCISE IS good for both your brain and your body because it boosts the part of your brain that helps you learn and remember. You can also exercise your brain by learning new things and doing brain-teasers, such as word and picture puzzles. Smoking and doing drugs can harm your brain, so you should not do them.

STAY HEALTHY
Eating lots of fresh fruit and vegetables keeps your body and brain healthy. Strawberries and leafy green vegetables are especially good because they contain substances that protect your brain cells.

Safety gear protects your brain and body during active sports.

Doctors use scanning machines to look inside a patient's brain. From the pictures on the screen, they can see problems developing and decide what treatment a patient needs.

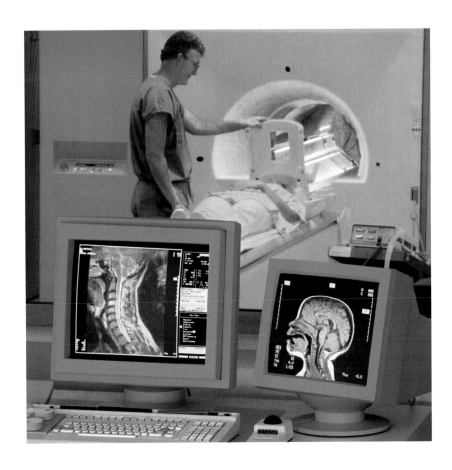

If someone damages one side of the brain, it affects the opposite side of the body. So if someone has a stroke in the left part of his brain, he may be unable to move the right side of his body. A stroke happens when a blood clot stops blood from reaching part of the brain.

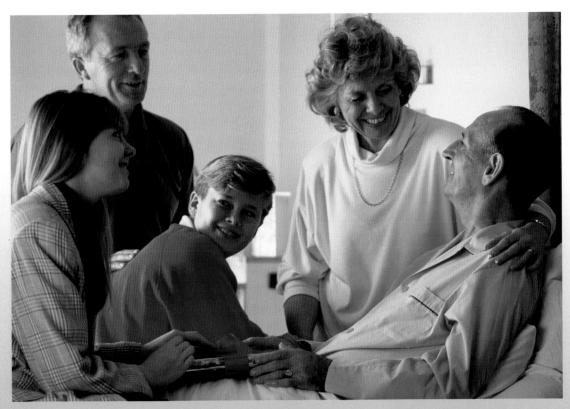

Glossary

adrenalin A hormone or chemical that your body produces when under pressure.

brain cell One of hundreds of billions of living units that together make up the brain.

brain stem The central core of the brain that is connected to the nerves in your spine.

cerebellum The part of the brain that controls coordination and balance.

cerebrum The largest part of the brain, which controls your senses.

cortex The outer layer of the brain.

digestive system The parts of the body that break food down so it is small enough to be absorbed.

emotions Strong feelings.

hormones Chemicals used to send signals around the body.

lungs Organs that you use for breathing.

memory A past action or event that is remembered.

motor center The part of the brain that controls the body's movement.

nerve A long strand of special cells that sends signals around the body.

nervous system The system made up of the brain, spinal cord, and nerves, which work together to let us touch, move, and feel.

pupils The small, round openings at the front of the eyes that let in light.

receptor A nerve ending in the skin that can feel sensations such as warmth, cold, and pain.

senses The five senses are sight, hearing, taste, smell, and touch. They give us information about the world around us and help protect us.

serotonin A chemical in your brain that affects your emotions.

sight center The part of the brain that senses sight.

skull The bones that protect your brain.

speech center The part of the brain that recognizes words and speech.

spinal cord A bundle of nerves that runs down the spine.

spine The string of small bones running down the back.

voice box The part of your throat where sound is produced.

Useful information

Books

Angliss, Sarah. *The Controls: Brain and Nervous System*. Thameside Press, 1999.

Bryan, Jenny. *Your Amazing Brain*. Westport, Conn.: Wishing Well Books, 1996.

Fitzpatrick, Anne. *The Brain*. North Mankato, Minn.: Smart Apple Media, 2003.

Web sites

<u>www.howstuffworks.com/brain.htm</u>
Information on how the brain works.

<u>www.brainpop.com/health/nervous/</u>
Information on the brain and nervous system.

<u>www.kidshealth.org/kid/body/brain/</u>
Information on how the brain and body work together.

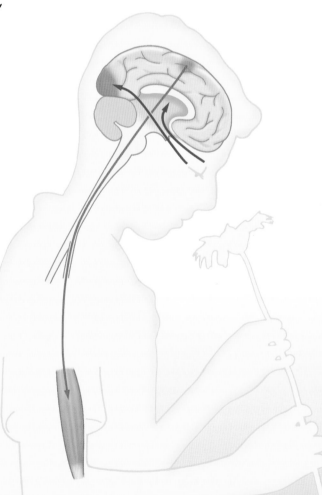

Index